KU-368-429

Wheels and Cogs

written by Caroline Rush
and
illustrated by Mike Gordon

HODDER
Wayland

Schools Library and Information Services

S00000668765

Simple Science

Wheels and Cogs
Slopes

Levers
Pulleys

DUDLEY PUBLIC LIBRARIES

L 47437

668765   SCH

J 531.8

Series Editor: Catherine Baxter

Advice given by Philip Cornish

First published in Great Britain in 1996
by Wayland (Publishers) Ltd
This edition printed in 2001 by Hodder Wayland,
an imprint of Hodder Children's Books

© Hodder Wayland 1996

British Library Cataloguing in Publication Data

Rush Caroline

    Wheels and cogs. – (Simple Technology Series)

    I. Title II. Gordon, Mike III. Series

    535.6

ISBN 0-7502-3410-5

Typeset by MacGuru

Printed and bound in Italy by G Canale and C.S.p.A., Turin, Italy

Contents

Wheels help things to move.
They come in all sizes and
colours.

But they are all the same shape.

Before wheels were invented, people had to drag heavy loads across the ground by pushing or pulling. This was hard work!

Then someone had the bright idea of using treetrunks as rollers. This made moving things around easier.

Try this simple experiment.

You will need:
2 shoe boxes

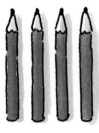

4 pencils
2 weights (the same)
a piece of chalk

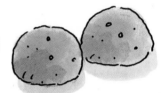

Stage 1
1. Put a weight in each shoebox.
2. Chalk a start line on a table top.

3. Put one box at the line. Push the box.
4. Mark the point where the box stops.

Stage 2
1. Lay the second box on the pencil rollers at the start line. Push this box.
2. Mark the point where the box stops.

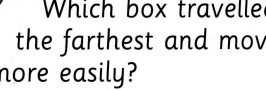

Which box travelled the farthest and moved more easily?

Rollers were the first kind of wheels that people used. Later they cut slices off the rollers to make sets of wheels, which would turn more easily on rough ground.

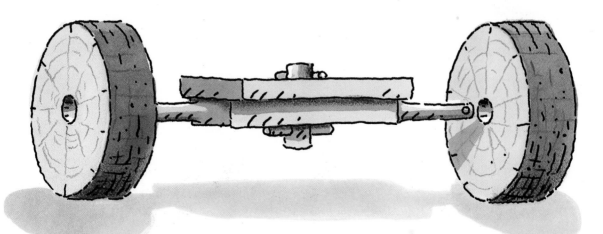

These were joined to an axle and were used to make the first carts. Moving things around was now even easier.

Make your own wheeled cart. You will need:

scissors

a glass

a shoebox

2 pencils

plasticine

sticky tape

corrugated cardboard

1. Use the glass to draw four cardboard wheels. With the help of a grown-up, cut the wheels out.

2. Punch a hole in their centres using a sharp pencil.

3. Make two pairs of holes in the sides of your shoebox. Be careful to line the pairs up or your cart will wobble!

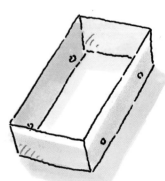

4. Slip a wheel on one end of a pencil.

5. Push the other end of the pencil through one pair of holes. Put a wheel on it.

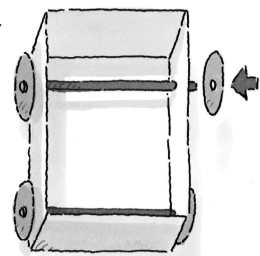

6. Repeat with the other pencil.

7. Tape the ends of the pencils to stop the wheels falling off.

Now test your cart!

One problem with the first wheels was they were heavy because they were made of solid wood.
It was difficult for vehicles to move quickly.

The Romans made the wheel lighter by cutting out the solid wood in the centre, and adding spokes. Vehicles could now go faster.

You still find some modern wheels that are similar to the wheels Romans designed. The centre of the wheel is called the hub.

Spokes join the hub to the rim (the outside of the wheel). The axle fits into the hub, and the wheel turns on the axle.

Many wheels have tyres around the outer rim. Tyres are made from rubber and steel. Tyres have a pattern in the rubber called a tread which grips the surface the wheel is travelling along.

Some tyres have a special tread.

The tyres of a tractor stop the wheels sinking into soft earth.

Different wheels are designed to do different jobs. Lorries have big wide wheels because they have to carry heavy loads.

Bicycle wheels have fine spokes that are very light, so the bicycle can go fast.

Look at the wheels around you. How do they suit the job they do?

Some wheels are called cogs or gearwheels. They have 'teeth' around the outside. The teeth of the cogs can mesh: when you turn just one wheel, other wheels turn too!

Make a set of cogs.

You will need:
a shoebox lid
two split pins
cardboard

1. Use template 1 on page 29 to cut out two identical cardboard cogs.
2. Fasten one to the shoebox lid with a split pin. The cog must be loose enough to turn.
3. Place the other cog next to the first, so that the teeth mesh. Fasten it to the lid.
4. Turn one of the cogs. Can you see the other cog turn too?

All sorts of everyday machines use cogs.

When you pedal a bicycle, you turn a large cog. This is attached by a chain to a smaller cog that turns the wheels. The cogs move energy from the pedals to the wheels.

With the help of a grown-up, put a bicycle upside down and slowly turn the pedal. Which moves faster, the big cog or the little cog, the pedal or the wheel?

Use templates 1 and 2 on page 29 to join a large cog to a small cog. (Follow the steps on page 23.)

When the cogs are in position draw a line on each cog at '12 o'clock'.

Look at the lines to find out how many times the smaller cog turns for every time the big cog turns.

Glossary

Axle   The shaft or rod on which a wheel turns.

Cog   A toothed gearwheel.

Energy   The power to do work.

Hub   The centre of a wheel.

Load   The weight of the object that is moved by a machine.

Pedal   A lever you press with your foot.

Rim   The outer edge of a wheel.

Spoke   Bars or rods which run from the centre to the rim of a wheel.

Tread   The pattern of grooves on a tyre which helps it to grip the road.

Tyre   A rubber hoop which fits around the rim of a wheel.

Templates for pages 23/27

1. Trace or photocopy
   these shapes.
2. Glue them to some card.
3. Cut them out.
4. Bend the tabs.

5. Pin the shapes to a piece
   of card.

Notes for adults

Simple Technology is a series of elementary books designed to introduce children to the everyday machines which make all of our lives easier, and the basic principles behind them.

For millions of years people have been inventing and using machines to make work easier. These machines have been constantly modified and redesigned over the years to make them more sophisticated and more successful at their task. This is really what technology is all about. It is the process of applying knowledge to make work easier. In these books, children are encouraged to explore the early inspirations for machines and the process of modification which has brought them forward to their current state, and in so doing, come to an understanding of the design process.

The simple text and humorous illustrations give a clear explanation of how these machines actually work and experiments and activities give suggestions for further practical exploration.

Suggestions for further activities

* Make a collection of wheels, including magazine cutouts and drawings of those around you. Discuss size and shape and how this relates to function.
* Encourage children to use lego and other construction kits to design and make wheeled vehicles. This kind of experimentation is an essential part of the design process.

* Introduce the fair test and encourage children to test out the models they make. Record, discuss and analyse the results of these tests.
* Encourage children to identify a design need and respond to this by designing on paper, constructing and testing out a model vehicle, which can then be modified and improved upon.
* Explore the principle of friction and how this affects movement along a surface. Test out vehicles on different surfaces. Record and analyse results.
* Design and make a model which uses cogs to move energy from one part of a machine to another.

Books to read

Starting Technology/Wheels by John Williams (Wayland, 1990)
The Way It Works/Motion by P. Sauvain (Heinemann, 1991)
Experiment With Movement by Brian Murphy (Watts, 1991)
The Story Of The Wheel by Tim Healey (Eagle Books, 1993)
Readabout Wheels by Henry Pluckrose (Watts, 1991)
Simple Science/Push and Pull by M. Gordon (Wayland, 1995)

Adult Reference
The Way Things Work by David Macaulay
(Dorling Kindersley, 1988)

Index